Folk Kilns II

FAMOUS CERAMICS OF JAPAN 4

Folk Kilns II

Kichiemon Okamura

KODANSHA INTERNATIONAL LTD.
Tokyo, New York, San Francisco

distributed in the United States by Kodansha International/USA, Ltd.,
through Harper & Row, Publishers, Inc., 10 East 53rd Street,
New York, New York 10022

published by Kodansha International Ltd., 12–21 Otowa 2–chome,
Bunkyo-ku, Tokyo 112 and Kodansha International/USA, Ltd., 10 East
53rd Street, New York, New York 10022 and 44 Montgomery Street,
San Francisco, California 94104

LCC 80–84463
ISBN 0–87011–477–8
JBC 1072–789642–2361

Folk Kilns of Kyushu, Shikoku, and Okinawa

The Beauty of Folk Wares

The term *mingei*, literally meaning "popular art," but generally translated into English as "folkcraft," was coined by the scholar and critic Muneyoshi (Sōetsu) Yanagi (1889–1961) and two potter friends, Kanjirō Kawai and Shōji Hamada, during the late 1920s. These three men formed the nucleus of what later came to be called the folkcraft movement. With remarkably good taste, they selected various crafts and pottery pieces from among articles used by ordinary people in their everyday lives—objects that until that time had been not just ignored but virtually despised. The term *mingei*, therefore, is an aesthetic concept, and does not refer to all everyday utensils. Yanagi coined phrases to express the *mingei* concept; some of these may be translated as "healthy beauty," "artless beauty," "frugal beauty," and "unobstructed beauty," though the English does not fully capture the meaning of the Japanese.

Folk pottery consists of various kinds of domestic kitchen wares—crocks, jars, large bowls, saké bottles, and so on. These wares possess a natural dignity that stems from the combination of three things: the *materials* used both to make and to fire the pottery; the craftsman's technical *skill*; and the *use* to which such pots are put. Although one kiln may differ from another, producing wares with slightly different forms, folk wares all have one thing in common: they are imbued with a vivacious beauty, whether they be made in Nishijin, Koishiwara, Onta, Shōdai, Ōsotoyama, Naeshirogawa, Ryūmonji, or Tsuboya. There is a sense of stability about these pots that can come only from honest workmanship born out of the environment in which the potter lives. Yet, at the same time, this stability comes only from years of trial and error, and it may be many decades before a certain technique is adopted as part of a kiln's tradition. There are, of course, all sorts of glazing and decorative techniques—some wares are plain and unglazed, others glazed in black, brown, or white, yet others decorated with polychrome glazes and enamels—but the very richness of their beauty derives in large part from the fact that they make use of natural materials. Potters may produce pots that are openhearted, quiet, or even melancholic. Yet *mingei* pots are never pretentious, by definition. Folkcraft wares contain within them a beauty that stems from man's humanity and from his struggle to survive.

Most folkcraft wares—like those made at Naeshirogawa, for example—are plain and simple. One can find more decorative pots, however, such as those produced at Ōsotoyama or Tsuboya, where polychrome overglaze enamel painting has been practiced. Such a decorative tradition is typical of Imari porcelain, its particular characteristic being stylized designs born from years of experience in brush painting. And yet this decorative technique does not remain just on the surface of the pot, but somehow manages to melt into and become an essential part of the clay body. Painting is something learned not by just the hand but by the whole body; thus a good craftsman need not rely on a rough outline of what he is going to paint, but can simply paint the desired decoration without such aids. Many of the decorated pieces that have survived to this day were painted by old women and children. They probably did not enjoy their work, but they still managed to paint quite beautifully. We who have been brought up in a different age with different conceptions of work and beauty may find this hard to understand, but we would do well to learn from the profound difference in attitude between ourselves and our forebears.

Firing the kiln is the climax of the various stages of pottery production. Basically, there are two methods of firing a kiln—oxidation and reduction. Each influences glaze chemistry, and thus pot colors, in its own way. In oxidation (also referred to as an oxidizing atmosphere), there is plenty of oxygen during firing, while with a reduction firing (reducing atmosphere), there is much smoke and little oxygen in the kiln chamber. One characteristic of folk pottery is that most wares are fired in a neutral firing, neither oxidizing nor reducing. Much of the beauty of the pots derives not so much from the potter's skill at producing an oxidation or reduction firing, but from his letting the kiln do the work and fire the pots the way *it* wants to.

Other features of folk wares are that in some cases potters do not bother to refine their clay before using it on the wheel; also, they may not give their pots a bisque firing, but instead glaze the green pots. Both of these practices can lead to a fairly high percentage of pots lost in the kiln, which in this age of modern technology many people would regard as economic suicide. At the same time, however, the fact that some potters work in one way and others in another way gives *mingei* pottery as a whole a great variety and stops it from becoming monotonous.

Folk pottery is for the most part made by traditional methods of production. This means that every kiln has at hand the basic raw materials of clay, water, and wood to fuel the kilns. In others words, in folkcrafts—and indeed in all traditional crafts—the craftsman brings together three essential factors: nature (environment and materials), the human aspect (use, economics, aesthetics), and technical skill. One can go further and say that the use to which a pot is put determines its form; the form influences the techniques with which it is made; and the techniques relate to the materials used. To put it another way, the nature of the materials defines the techniques that can be used make a pot. The way in which the craftsman makes things for ordinary use may communicate a real sense of vitality in the objects that he produces.

The history of ceramics in general begins with, and develops from, the fact that pots are made to be used. Folk potteries stand at the very core of this history, for they are primarily concerned with the production of everyday wares. Among such potteries one can make a distinction between those that produce glazed porcelain and stoneware and those that fire unglazed earthenware and roof tiles; in other words, between kilns producing high- and low-fired wares.

Dark and Light Wares

Japanese pottery is usually classified into dark and light, or "black" and "white," wares. The former term refers to stoneware with a dark glaze; this gives a sense of informality and stops dirt from showing. Sometimes these have brightly colored overglazes, which contrast with the gloomy, dark kitchens common to old Japanese homes. It may well be that the Japanese passion for poured glazes, and for colors that have come out somewhat unexpectedly because of accidents during kiln firing, has something to do with their general sentimentality. Certainly, there are few folk wares elsewhere in the world that make such liberal use of overglaze techniques. Potteries in the west of Japan in particular—for instance, Koishiwara, Ryūmonji, Shōdai, and Tsuboya—make a lot of these "black" wares.

Light, "white" wares came to be made as a result of the spread of porcelain techniques, which became widely known for the most part in the latter half of the nineteenth century. In some cases, however, these techniques were adopted by folk potteries as early as the middle of the eighteenth century. Within the Japanese folkcraft tradition, "white" ware generally refers to the use of white slip as a means of coating a dark stoneware clay body. For the most part, big commercial kilns in places like Ōsotoyama were the first to make use of bright, warm, opaque slip clay. Very few pots were left entirely undecorated. Rather, they were painted with iron or cobalt underglazes and then given finger-wipe decorations to produce pieces unsurpassed by those from any kiln in the country. Brushed slip (*hakebiki*), brush-tapped slip (*uchibake*), and chatter-marking were among the many decorative techniques adopted.

Porcelain

Porcelain is generally regarded as having been introduced into Japan via Korea. Although written records make no mention of the fact, one should recognize that—so far as folk pottery is concerned—a parallel strain came into the country from southern China. This should be taken into account if certain inconsistencies are to be avoided.

In comparison with stoneware, porcelain is relatively expensive. Consequently, it should be assumed any porcelain wares made for everyday use at, a folk kiln probably developed about half a century after stoneware production was initiated. While there are instances of porcelain not being bisqued before the main firing (such as with Old Imari ware), this could hardly have been the case with folk porcelain produced in the Ōmura clan fief, which stretched from Arita to Hirado in present-day Nagasaki Prefecture. Most of that ware was fired at a slightly lower temperature than is normal for porcelain, and the clay body was decorated with stamping and quiet cobalt brushwork. The latter decoration reached a peak between the Empō and Kansei eras (1673–1801). It was only after this that local porcelain kilns, such as at Tobe, on Shikoku, came into their own.

The Establishment of Folk Potteries

It is almost impossible to tell precisely when folk pottery kilns were established, but it can generally be assumed that they became significant once ceramic production began to spread throughout Japan, during the early stages of the Edo period (1603–1868). Prior to the last decade of the sixteenth century, wares somewhat North Korean in style were fired at the Kishidake kilns, east of Matsuura, while a few simple ash- or iron-glazed pots were made north of Arita at places like Yamabeta. The style of these latter wares appears to be Chinese in origin. Both types of pottery are important, since historically they were the forerunners of folk wares. They were not produced in response to a nationwide demand, however. So far as broad geographical divisions of style are concerned, one can say that Kyushu's folk pottery kilns were founded on a Korean stylistic tradition, primarily as a result of the warlord Toyotomi Hideyoshi's invasions of that country between 1592 and 1598. Kilns to the east of Kyushu, on Shikoku, for example, owe more to the influence of Kyoto wares.

All crafts, but particularly folkcrafts, have both functional and economic aspects of production. Folk potteries in the west of Japan, such as those at Shii-no-mine, Ōsotoyama, and Kiwarayama, were fairly large-scale kilns with a wide distribution network, so that from as early as the first decade of the seventeenth century they started producing unglazed grinding bowls (suribachi) as standard ware. There is very little written documentation of the history of these kilns, and some facts can only be inferred from what has been inscribed on potters' gravestones, but it would seem that Shii-no-mine was the center of both technical advances and production until it went into decline at the very end of the eighteenth century.

Potteries that fired wares to meet a small-scale regional demand are known in Japanese as "local" kilns (jigama), and one can see from shards unearthed at old kiln sites that places like Koishiwara and Ryūmonji in fact developed in much the same way as the larger kilns mentioned above. These local kilns were mostly patronized and supervised by the clan authorities of the fiefs in which they were located. At first they made special pots to order for the clan lord, in addition to folk wares; later they turned to satisfying local demand, which increased considerably up to the end of the eighteenth century, and produced a large quantity of everyday utensils. Once more, there is unfortunately little in the way of written documentation to show just how market demand was satisfied.

So far as distribution is concerned, almost all the large urns and jars known today were fired in these local folk potteries. When the system of feudal fiefs was abolished late in the nineteenth century and the present prefectural administration system was set up in its stead, potters lost the patronage of the clan authorities and consequently turned to the production of everyday wares for the local populace. This much is known. What is unclear, however—mainly as a result of a lack of written records and of the high rate of consumption—is how pottery was distributed prior to the nineteenth century. It is therefore extremely difficult to construct any sort of detailed chronology, but a general statement can be made to the effect that folk potteries were in their infancy during the first four decades of the seventeenth century, became established in the 1660s, flourished between 1688 and 1735, and reached a point of stable production thereafter, before beginning to fade away during the latter half of the nineteenth century. Almost all local kilns would appear to have gone through these four phases.

The Japanese folkcraft movement has led to the establishment of a number of new folk potteries. Muneyoshi Yanagi and other leaders of the movement during the late 1920s and the 1930s discovered many folk kilns and helped a number of them to revive production. Some of these potteries were well known; others were not. It so happened that the folkcraft movement arose at an extremely important stage in the development of Japanese aesthetics. It was a cultural movement, based on a philosophy advocating a recognition of hitherto neglected objects, and while the mingei concept might be difficult to grasp in all its applications, there was urgent need to select genuinely beautiful craftwork at that time to present an image and working model of *mingei*. The impetus that Yanagi gave to folk-crafts in general led to the emergence of a number of new potteries, but these are currently still going through an initial period of confusion and have not as yet settled down to producing really good works.

Okinawa Prefecture

Tsuboya is the most important pottery on the main island of Okinawa, established by Korean potters (known in Japanese as Ichiroku, Ikkan, and Sankan) who were invited there from Satsuma during the Genna period (1615–24). Although some pots were made for the Okinawan royal household, most of Tsuboya's wares were for everyday use and included crocks, saké bottles and cups, large and small bowls, dishes, and cinerary vessels, symmetrically shaped gourd saké bottles, hip flasks, and flower vases. Of these, the cinerary vessels and the crescent-shaped hip flasks have been fired in some quantity and have become the hallmark of Okinawan ware. Pots are decorated in a variety of ways—trailing, polychrome under- and overglaze painting, inlay, sprigging, incised relief—while some pots are slipped and left undecorated. Several other potteries existed (at Chibana, for example, where unglazed wares were fired in large numbers; and at Kina, Wakita, and Takaraguchi) before the Tsuboya kiln was established. There was also another, really old, kiln at Kogachi, where traces of South China pottery techniques can be seen.

Glazed wares are known in Okinawa as *jōyaki* (high-class wares), and these harmonize well with the deep blue of the south sea skies in the way that they are strongly built and brightly decorated with colorful designs. The iron-rich clay body is covered with a white slip; ash-based glazes are made from rice-straw ash mixed with coral, to which are added proportions of iron and copper; opaque green and purplish blue glazes are also found. Some of the pottery is made on the kick wheel, but some of it is made in molds from slabs, with modeling and pinching. Every workshop has now turned to full-time production, but in the old days pots were made by families working independently, and one could come across children dabbing glazes onto pots with their fingers, or pouring them from cupped leaves.

Unglazed pots are called *namban* and are made by a method of coiling and paddling still encountered in potteries in central and northern parts of Thailand. There were kilns on other islands besides Okinawa—Taketomi, Aragusuku, and Yonaguni, for example—but these no longer produce. The tradition of making a Chinese type of tile is carried on at Miyara and Hateruma, which produce brightly colored everyday wares, as well as lion-shaped tile guardian figures that are put on the roofs of houses. They also fire red, Mediterranean style, cylindrical tiles that are reminiscent of tiles produced during the Nara period (710–794).

Kyushu

Kyushu has since the Yayoi period (300 B.C.–A.D. 250) directly taken in various foreign cultural influences. Following Hideyoshi's invasions of the Korean peninsula in the 1590s, the north of the island became one gigantic pottery complex, for a large number of Korean potters was brought back by Japanese daimyo. Just as Seto and Mino are the main centers of pottery production for the east of Japan, so is Kyushu that in the west of the country. The interesting thing to note here is that while the word for pottery in the east of Japan is *setomono*, taking its name from the most important center of pottery production there (Seto), in Kyushu and west Japan the word commonly used for pottery is *karatsu*. This term derives not from the name of a kiln, but from that of the port (Karatsu) from which pottery was shipped. However, highly decorative porcelain is called Imari ware, because Imari was the port that serviced the Arita porcelain kilns. A further contrast between the two areas of Japan can be found in the fact that folk wares in the east of the country are influenced by ancient kilns and developed around the production of unglazed and untrimmed plates and shallow grating dishes; those made in Kyushu, on the other hand, started with unglazed grinding bowls, which derived from Korea. The Kyushu wheel is in general kicked in a counterclockwise direction (except for trimming) and this again contrasts with the clockwise turning wheel found in the east of Japan.

Kagoshima Prefecture

Naeshirogawa. The distinction between "black" and "white" wares has already been discussed. What are known as Black Satsuma (Satsuma being the name of the feudal fief; roughly the same area as modern Kagoshima Prefecture) wares have been fired continuously in Kagoshima since the very end of the sixteenth century. Many dynamic works exist that have been made by Korean techniques, and Naeshirogawa is the purest example of this traditional type of stoneware. When the Korean potters first landed in Japan after Hideyoshi's invasions of their country, they built a kiln at Kushikino, but soon moved to the present site of Mikawa. At present two kilns are being fired there, although remains of other cooperative kiln sites may be found at Motoyashiki and Tamachi.

Iron glazes have been used throughout the pottery's long history, and these give such colors as buckwheat gray, rust red, brown, yellow ochre, blue, and red. Pots that have been glazed with a mixture using a local iron-bearing sand dug from a nearby river bed are called *kogare* (burnt) in the local dialect. Various kinds of decoration are used—sprigging, incised relief, and combing—and a large number of different shapes and sizes of ware are made—*choka* pots, jars, crocks, pouring vessels, cooking pots, all sorts of grinding, pouring, rice, and other bowls, dishes, small handled teapots (*kyūsu*), even farm implements. Some unglazed wares were also produced. *Choka* are vessels for local, strong distilled spirits and can be found in various shapes, some shallow and with two spouts, others for use by farmers in the fields, yet others that were intended for everyday use in the home. "Sweet-saké" jars with modeled images of Daikoku-sama, the god of wealth, and *umebachi* flower bowls with sprigged-on flower, pine, and rope decorations are characteristic of Naeshirogawa's superb workmanship.

Ryūmonji. Like Naeshirogawa, this pottery was also started at the end of the sixteenth century, but the kiln site was moved several times before potters settled in Oyamada during the Kyōhō period (1716–35). The kiln that was fired there until before the Pacific War has been preserved and can be seen by the workshop, where it serves as a reminder of the past. Nowadays, Ryūmonji ware consists of brightly slipped bowls, rice bowls, saké bottles, and other containers, which have brown and green dripped glazes. Green-glazed covered dishes with white glaze pours are also made. The decorations found on shards around the old kiln sites are almost identical to Ōsotoyama or Koishiwara wares in the way they are inlaid with slip or have *hakeme* and combed decorations.

Hirasa. Hirasa Sarayama was a center of porcelain production, potters having come here from Arita in the 1720s and made cobalt-decorated and plain white porcelain wares for everyday use—cups, saké bottles, rice bowls, and teapots, along with square-shouldered saké bottles that were exported abroad and had writing on them in Roman letters.

Tanegashima. Two kiln sites have been discovered on this island, and the shards unearthed there show that wares with iron and brownish red glazes were fired here, just like those made at Naeshirogawa, as well as unglazed crocks and jars, kneading bowls, and saké bottles.

Kumamoto Prefecture

Shōdai. There is a kiln called Kōda, which produced excellent inlaid pots at Yatsushiro, but the best-known folk pottery is that found at Shōdai. During the Genna period (1615–24) two potters, Hin-no-Kōji and Katsuragi, moved from Agano to Shōdai and started making wares with opaque running glazes. Besides firing pots to order for the clan lord of the area, they also filled the demand for such domestic wares as water crocks, tea jars, saké bottles, and kneading bowls, and many really superb kitchen utensils (but not cooking vessels) were produced. Potters working in Shōdai adopted a number of Korean stoneware techniques and adapted them to suit Japanese taste. A large number of marvelous works survive to this day, richly glazed in white, amber, and *namako* (purplish blue). Two kilns continued producing Shōdai wares until early in this century, before going out of business. Following the end of the Pacific War, however, a new kiln was built again at Fumoto, and everyday wares have been fired there using the same traditional glazing techniques. This is, therefore, an important *mingei* kiln.

Nagasaki Prefecture

The most important Nagasaki potteries are those found at Hasami and Mikawachi, both of them mainly producing porcelain. In the old days these wares were generally classified as Imari for two reasons. First, the clay and decorative methods used were virtually identical with, and hence indistinguishable from, Old Imari wares. Second, the clan lord of the fief in which Hasami was situated used to ship Hasami wares from the port of Imari. A distinction could be made between Hasami and Mikawachi wares in that the latter were shipped from the port of Hirado and not from

Imari, but the situation is somewhat complicated by the fact that the two potteries produced wares that were so similar in style.

Hasami. The first kiln was built at Hatanohara, but it was rebuilt at Sannomata once potters, led by one Ri Yūkei, found more suitable materials. From there they gradually moved downstream along the Toishi River, building kilns at Sannomata Hongama, Seiji, Kibayama, Kōrai, Nakao Honnobori, Nagao Hongama. Another kiln can be found along the Kawatana River (of which the Toishi is a tributary) at Uchinomi. All of these produced wares for everyday use—*kurawanka* bowls, plates, saké bottles, various shapes and sizes of rice bowl, noodle sauce and tea cups, etc. Many of the plates were stamped with floral impressions.

The name *kurawanka* comes from the fact that this crude porcelain bowl was hawked to people drinking aboard boats on the Yodo River in Osaka. They were invited in the local dialect to "drink some saké" from these bowls (*saké kurawan ka?*), which were generously decorated in cobalt with a high iron content and glazed with an ash glaze. The foot rim is small and trimmed away at the center to look rather like a pointed helmet. Not many motifs were used to decorate these bowls—floral scrolls, plum and rock, cherry, maple, pine and lattice—and they were mainly fired only in the valley kilns of Sannomata, Nakao, and Nagao. At any rate, these bowls suddenly ceased being made from about the second decade of the eighteenth century.

In the folk potteries, cobalt underglazing underwent various changes; the clay became whiter; pots were made thinner. Yet, at the same time the designs lost much of their power as they became more elaborate. One design that did continue for a very long time was that of the lattice.

Mikawachi. One of the centers of production of the *kurawanka* bowls was at Enaga in Mikawachi, where a number of kilns were built. Two particularly striking characteristics of the Mikawachi wares are that oil jars were produced along with bowls and dishes, and the use of stamped designs increased noticeably. The fact that "morning glory" bowl forms were called "Canton" in Kyushu is evidence of Chinese ceramic influence in the region. Mikawachi wares were in fact connected with early Harayake and Mukunodani wares, but Tengudani wares are characterized by a different Chinese stylistic strain.

Kiwarayama. Across the mountain range to the east of Enaga and adjoining Arita is the region of Kiwarayama, in which a number of kilns may be found—Yanagi-no-moto, Yoshi-no-moto, An-no-mae, and Jizōdaira. This is an important center of old folk potteries, where semiporcelain was fired from fairly early on. It is, however, difficult to distinguish these bowls and saké bottles with their cobalt underglaze landscape and floral scroll motifs from Shii-no-mine wares. The style of decoration is known as *sotowa Karatsu* and includes a freely brushed *hakeme* effect, which is linked to that used in Kodaji and was adopted by potters working in Utsutsugawa.

Saga Prefecture

Shii-no-mine. Saga Prefecture boasts a large number of kilns that have made and fired wares typical of western Japan. One of these may be found at Shii-no-mine, which was started by a fairly large number of potters who came to Japan following Hideyoshi's invasions of Korea (1592–98). Together they set up an enormous pottery complex, which consisted of more than 350 households. There are a number of kiln sites remaining. At one of these, known as the Upper Tatara kiln, in Hotoke Valley, a lot of unglazed wares were fired; the Middle Tatara kilns in Nakasen Valley produced a number of different shaped wares glazed in a variety of colors; but it was the Lower Tatara kilns that developed the most eye-arresting techniques. An examination of shards from the kiln sites shows that early wares were decorated with mottled (*kobiki*) or *hakeme* decoration, while later pots were trailed or inlaid with slip. These techniques, and the use of various wood-ash glazes, together with a green glaze, formed the foundation of what later came to be conceived of as a particularly *mingei* style. One can follow the development of this style in the way in which first stencils, then slip combing and finger wipes, copper and iron brush painting, then glaze pouring all came to be adopted. The wide range of techniques used at the Lower Tatara kiln (Komadani Nakagama) are extremely beautiful.

In addition to the original Korean potters, other potters from China and also from Mino came to live and work here before returning to their own kilns. It was in this way that the techniques developed here were widely distributed. The pottery flourished for a century or more and reached its peak right at the end of the seventeenth century. Then, for some unknown reason, potters dispersed elsewhere, leaving only five households. The latter built a new kiln in which they fired mostly inlaid and soft-looking, iron-glaze decorated pieces. They formed the style now known as *sotowa Karatsu*, which relies on landscape and floral scroll designs for its effect.

Kanaishibaru. Between Shii-no-mine and Takeo may be found the two kiln sites of Fujin-gawachi and Kanaishibaru, where various opaque glazed wares were at one time produced. It was at Kanaishibaru that wares for everyday use were mainly fired, and the bowls, bottles, and dishes made here are particularly attractive. There are quite a lot of good *hakeme* decorated wares, and the round-bottomed teabowl form, customarily found in the San'in region, and particularly sonorous, came to Kanaishibaru via Shii-no-mine. The clay used has a high iron content and is extremely hard.

Ōsotoyama. Takeo Karatsu is a term used to describe a type of ware produced in the Takeo region, and, like the Lower Tatara kilns at Shii-no-mine, one can follow the process of its development very clearly. It is sometimes claimed that Takeo should be split into two regions and that pottery techniques spread from the northern to the southern region, but there seems little use in making such a distinction, for there is no basis for suggesting that northern Takeo wares are older than southern wares.

In fact, the term Takeo Karatsu is not used locally at all, and the phrase Ōsotoyama ware is preferred, for Ōsotoyama is indeed one enormous ceramic melting pot of styles and traditions. Most of the kiln sites are to be found in the cryptomeria (*sugi*) forests and orange orchards bordering the undulating mountain ranges in Fujitsu County. Very few of these appear to have fired tea ceremony wares exclusively, and there are several ordinary folk pottery kilns as well—these probably having been administered by clan authorities and local civilians. They thus should be seen as essentially in the folkcraft tradition, producing wares for everyday use by the local populace.

At the very center of Ōsotoyama can be found the kiln of Uchida Kotōge, where a large number of rustic-looking *mishima* Karatsu wares were fired with sgraffito, *hakeme*, and inlay decoration. Apart from incised and stamped inlay of pine tree and floral motifs, there are some splendid slip-painted wares with camellia, plum, spiderwort, peony, night jar (*hototogisu*), flower basket, and field horsetail motifs. Other wares have very fine calligraphy decorations. Most pots made at this kiln for everyday use and exhibit excellent forms, whose strength lies particularly in the shape of the foot rim. The method of applying slip decoratively with a straw whisk (Plate 49) was also practiced, while bowls, plates, and dishes were frequently decorated with wave or floral impressed patterns, which give the wares a sense of informality. Very rarely, one comes across pots with just their rims dipped in slip. Various kinds of overglaze painting were also tried here, along with underglaze cobalt decoration. Unfortunately, no complete pots exist, but the kiln is renowned for its somewhat primitive yet elegant wares.

Taitani. Taitani pottery is well known for its marvelous slip decorations, which include many combed and finger-wipe motifs brightly overglazed in two colors. Some pots also have iron brush painting, which is charmingly thick and generous without being crude. Cobalt underglaze decorated wares were also fired at Taitani, but these are not as old as those produced at Kotōge.

Kuronda. Plain Karatsu wares, together with iron-painted bowls and saké bottles have been discovered at this kiln site. The old iron-glazed pouring bowls and teapots and saké bottles with dripped amber glaze over combing are superb. Pottery is still being made here.

Kawago. Kawago is famous for its really marvelous two-color Karatsu wares, many of them with incised decorations of grape, pine tree, reed, and pampas grass motifs. Other decorative techniques included *hakeme* and stenciling in white slip. Green Karatsu wares were also fired here. Three kiln sites have been discovered between the top and bottom of the Kawago Valley and, like the kilns at Taitani and Kotōge, they produced some powerful pieces of pottery. There are other kiln sites in the neighborhood. One of these, Yakiyama, fired a fine two-color Karatsu type of saké bottle with pine decoration. Shards unearthed at other sites show that two-color bowls with combed decorations were predominantly made.

Yumino is situated on a small mound overlooking the Ureshino-Takeo road. It was from here that the Futagawa kiln later branched, and Yumino pottery is well known for its large slip-coated kneading bowls made of iron-bearing clay. These are frequently decorated with dynamically painted designs of mountains and large pine tree branches, or woods against a mountain background. Even narrow-based jars have this kind of picture painted on them, at times with *torii* (Shintō gateways) and cranes added for good measure.

A number of kilns have been built over the years more or less on the same spot, and the shards unearthed from the deepest level consist of grinding bowls and smaller pouring bowls with stenciled slip decorations, reminiscent of Kotōge and Kawago wares. These kneading bowls were probably first made to use in processing wax, since this particular area of Kyushu was famous for its wax production. In due course, however, the bowls came to be put to wider use—for kneading buckwheat dough, for instance, in order to make noodles. It has recently been discovered that not only were these bowls sold widely throughout Japan, even north of Tokyo, but that they were exported to Southeast Asia. Pots were made light and thin, being expertly trimmed.

Although the demand for large kneading bowls fell once the demand for wax decreased, large crocks were fired for some considerable time thereafter, not in porcelain, which was much too difficult, but in stoneware. This was brightened by the use of white slip, and iron and copper green glazes came to be used in place of cobalt blue underglaze and the copper red glaze associated with porcelain wares.

Shirakibara. There are three old kiln sites at Shirakibara, situated in a bamboo grove in the village of Kodaji, not too far from Yumino. Some wares found here are unglazed, others have an undecorated but slipped clay body with copper glaze, in two-color Karatsu style. An examination of shards unearthed at these kiln sites show that while the pieces have good, sharp forms, they are not very large, suggesting that the kilns were being fired prior to the demand for wax kneading bowls. These pots are decorated with grape, reed, pine and butterfly motifs, and iron brushwork was also used. Shirakibara's particular characteristic is the medium-sized (20 centimeter diameter) dishes in which a floral stamp has been impressed on the high, roughly trimmed foot rims. These have been glazed with *tenmoku* black (or, rarely, inlaid) over which copper glaze is applied. Iron-glazed and combed pieces as well as green Karatsu ware were also fired at Shirakibara, a kiln of age and status.

Kashinoki-yama. On the other side of the road from Shirakibara lies the kiln of Kashinoki-yama, where a large number of rather soft-looking *hakeme* decorated bowls, plates, and crocks have been unearthed. Stylistically, these would appear to be the forerunners of the *mishima* Karatsu and Utsutsugawa wares. White slip was frequently poured in two-color style, and many pots were decorated with the straw whisk type of *hakeme*.

Both the Yazaa and Shimomatsu valleys are near Kodaji village, and a lot of really good pots have been discovered in Shimomatsu. Two-color Karatsu and green Karatsu wares are quite hard to distinguish from pots fired at either Yumino or Shirakibara. It has been suggested that pottery was also fired at a place called Niwagi, but nobody has ever found any traces of old kiln sites there.

Right in the depths of the Takeo region can be found the kiln site of Teikibara, where large kneading bowls were made and fired. These were slipped before being decorated with a lattice pattern of combing and applied with two-color glaze pours. The fine combing used has been called a kind of clay feathering (*uzurade*), but this method of decoration was actually used to stop the white slip from peeling from the clay body. Old two-glazed kneading bowls should generally be thought of as having been fired in Teikibara.

Ōsotoyama encompasses all the above-mentioned potteries. Stretching north as far as Kawago and south to Uchinoyama, it lies on a large stratum of clay used by all the kilns producing Ōsotoyama ware. There is little white clay (for slip), and it was dug at the Sakura Pass in the north near Kuronda, and at Niwagi and Umekihara in the south. In the early period (approximately 1603–70), slip was fairly thickly applied and simply decorated. As time went by, however, it was gradually thinned, and abstract sgraffito decorations were applied. By the mid nineteenth century, the slip had become much thicker once again. The kilns were started during the first decade of the seventeenth century and flourished during the 1690s. The number of kilns around places like Yumino, Kodaji, and Niwagi suggests that potters working in this area moved around quite a bit. They also appear to have fired some porcelain wares.

Tatarō. Taku, to the east of Takeo, is famous for its special iron glaze, which gives a rather somber look to Taku Karatsu ware. Several potteries are known to have existed there, but then the Taku Karatsu style spread westwards through the Sabi Valley to Tatarō, and thence to Kamino. Pots were made by the coil-and-throw method, before being pressed from the inside with a shaping tool and paddled on the outside with a flat board. Tatarō is the only place where this technique is still in use. The clay body is rough and thick, and pots are raw glazed with a rice-straw-ash glaze that looks similar to Irabo glaze. Sometimes they are so crude in appearance that they seem almost dull. All sorts of pots are made at Tatarō—funerary urns, water jars, bowls, grinding bowls, water bottles, hand warmers, flower vases, and so on—and when making very large pieces, potters adopted the same tactics as at the Ōtani kiln in Shikoku. One potter would lie on his back or side and turn the wheel, while the other formed the clay. This technique is no longer used.

Imari. It is a well-known story that the reason the feudal lord of Saga fief did not build a kiln at Imari during the Edo period (1603–1868) was that he was afraid that his technical secrets would be stolen by those involved in the buying and selling of pottery. Porcelain was thus made at Arita, and some of the early kilns that can be linked to folkcraft traditions are those at Shirakawa Tengudani, Hyakkan Kakenodani and Konabe. Nothing much is known about the first of these kilns, but at the other two the slightly earthy clay was decorated in cobalt underglaze with willow leaf, landscape, and net designs, many of these becoming the basis for later decorative techniques. Certainly, these early cobalt-decorated pieces have a free, spirited simplicity that is not just beautiful but makes the pots occupy a special place in the history of Imari porcelains.

Most porcelain kilns in and around Arita produced miscellaneous wares, and Kakiemon's famous kiln is no exception.

Shiraishi, near the border of Saga and Fukuoka prefectures is at present producing earthenware, but in the old days porcelain was produced and fired in this kiln (Sōha ware). Since the latter half of the nineteenth century, potters have glazed their earthenware pots with a red *raku* style glaze, adding amber and green and occasionally even dripped white glazes. Bright colored lidded jars, cooking pots, teapots, baking pans and dishes are made here.

Ōita Prefecture
Onta. Onta Sarayama is situated in the northwest of Ōita Prefecture, seventeen kilometers from the town of Hita and across the mountains from Koishiwara, from where a potter came and set up a kiln in 1705. To this very day one can still hear the sound of the water-powered clay crushers that line the two streams running through the community. The clay is very similar to that used at Koishiwara, and pots are generally not bisque fired. A wide range of pottery is made at Onta, from very large water crocks and pickling jars to tiny *uruka* salted fish pots. All sorts and sizes of lidded jars, kneading and grinding bowls, pouring bowls, saké bottles, pitchers, teabowls, dishes, and rice bowls are made. Decorative techniques consist of appliqué, three-color overglazing, sgraffito, *hakeme*, combing, and finger wipes, and it was from here that Koishiwara potters learned the art of chatter-marking (Plate 56). Black, brown, and green glazes are used in various combinations, and often one or two glazes are poured over a transparent glazed *hakeme* (brushed slip) pattern (Plate 57). Although the pottery nowadays looks quite bright, in the old days wares were stronger and more somber, like the pots made in Koishiwara.

Fukuoka Prefecture
Agano. Agano wares were first produced in the Keichō period (1596–1614), being fired in a kiln situated at Kokura, in the northeast of Kyushu. Agano ware is famous for its tea ceremony objects, but everyday utensils have also been made, and all sorts of slip techniques have been used for decorative purposes, including overglaze trailing, sgraffito, and combing. Agano ware was fired in various kilns until about the middle of the nineteenth century, but it is no longer made. In the early period, iron, wood, and rice-straw-ash glazes were used; later on a green glaze was trailed over a white ash glaze to produce what is now commonly accepted and known as Agano ware. In addition to these glazes, a rather pleasantly fresh three-color glaze combination was also used. One of the better-known types is a rather bony looking saké bottle with very fine trailed lines of slip on its neck and a slip-trailed wave design on its body.

Nishijin. Nishijin is one of the kilns, which, along with Agano, produces the famous Takatori style tea wares, but it also makes folk pottery known as Nishiyama ware. The kiln was started in the Kyōhō period (1716–35) by a potter who came from Koishiwara (see below). As a result it has, in fact, no direct link with Takatori tea wares. The clay used is very fine and slightly dark, and it is frequently and liberally glazed with three-color glazes (Plate 58), thus leading one to believe that Nishiyama ware owes more to Agano than to Koishiwara in stylistic tradition. A transparent purplish blue (*namako*) and black (*kameguro*) glaze are also used on various kinds of pottery—crocks, jars, bowls, teapots, pouring vessels, miniature shrines, and so on. These glazes are thick and give the somewhat hard-looking clay body a dignified ambience.

Another pottery that, like Nishijin, could be found right in the heart of Fukuoka city was Noma. Here casseroles, lidded jars, teapots, and black-and-white checkered cooking pots used to be fired. They were made from a light, *raku*-ware type of earthenware clay and were glazed in white, black, and green.

Koishiwara. Koishiwara started out from its very beginning as a folk type of kiln producing wares for everyday use. Early pots consisted of thick, unglazed grinding bowls and jars, and very occasionally these were roughly combed and dipped in an ash glaze. Then the potters moved from Ipponsugi to the top of the present hamlet of Sarayama, with its line of water-powered clay crushers along the single mountain stream, and as many as ten different kilns were built over the years at Nakano and Kami-no-hara, but today the kilns have moved to Nakao.

From the middle of the eighteenth century, combing, *hakeme*, and other decorative slip techniques have been practiced, as well as glaze dripping, pouring, and trailing (*nagashi, uchikake, itchin*), together with modeling and wax resist decoration. New glazes—particularly brown and green glazes—were adopted and used with great success, giving the wares a slightly somber, heavy look. Their appearance was enlivened by the adoption of chatter-mark decoration in white slip early in this century. At that time, all kinds of pots were well thrown from a fine local clay into light forms. Some of them were for everyday, others for ritual use, and they included water urns, lidded jars, various kinds of bowls, plates, and saké bottles. Potters have traditionally glazed their wares in three colors over a white slip. Alternatively, they put in a chatter-mark decoration and add overglaze splashes. The large lidded pickling jars and knobless lidded tea jars are typical of Koishiwara ware, which also occasionally included a green-glazed teapot.

Futagawa. This pottery stemmed from Yumino (see under Saga Prefecture) during the late nineteenth century, and its wares are close in style to those of Ōsotoyama ware. The pots with pine tree designs are famous, but most pieces were slipped and given finger-wipe decorations. Water urns, crocks, kneading bowls, and lidded jars are most common, and these mainly in a running amber glaze. Futagawa is now the only folk pottery producing the Takeo Karatsu style of ware.

Shikoku

Shikoku is a large island, separated from the main island of Japan by the Inland Sea. Its southern shores are lapped by the Pacific Ocean's waves, and wide channels separate it from Ōita Prefecture to the west, on Kyushu, and from Wakayama Prefecture to the east, on Honshu. It has no ancient kilns, nor were any traditional techniques brought to the island by potters from Korea who arrived in Japan following Toyotomi Hideyoshi's invasions of that country in the last decade of the sixteenth century. All the kilns presently active on Shikoku were set up after the seventeenth century, when potters from Kyushu and the main island of Honshu decided to start working there.

Kagawa Prefecture

It is still possible to find country villages called by various Japanese terms for pottery—Doki, for example, meaning "earthenware," and Sue, "pottery." Although such names lead one to believe that these villages must have made ceramics at some stage in the past, none of them is, in fact, producing pottery now.

To the west of the city of Takamatsu is a place called Kōzai, where potters still eke out a living making herbal teapots and washbasins. Herbal teapots are made of refractory clay to allow them to be used directly on a naked flame in order to brew herbal infusions and heat water. The washbasins are glazed green, and some of them are extremely charming. In Kinashi, just to the south of Kōzai, two types of herbal teapot—one round, the other with a flange rim— are fired with a kind of red *raku* (lead) glaze.

There are a number of kilns along the coast between Yashima and Kan'onji where low-fired pottery is made from clay used primarily for roof tiles.

Mimaya, for example, produces casseroles, ember pots, frying pans, kettles, three-legged charcoal braziers, and mushroom steamers, all molded wares.

One of the most active kilns is that at Okamoto, where both large and small pots are wheel thrown—washbasins, barrels, cooking stoves, stools, bathtubs, and small pots, such as parching pans. In the past, several dozen kilns fired here along the main road into the town, and the pots are humble and rustic.

Ehime Prefecture

Roof tile clay wares are fairly widely produced in Ehime Prefecture, and frying pans, lidded cooking pots, cooking stoves, round well covers, and even household altar shrines have been fired there.

Tobe. Tobe is situated to the south of the city of Matsuyama, and cobalt underglaze decorated porcelain (blue-and-white) wares have been made there since the 1770s. It is known, however, from shards found at the Kitakawage kiln site, that stoneware was made prior to porcelain, but nowadays the name of Tobe is virtually synonymous with porcelain. Porcelain was first produced in Arita in northwest Kyushu, but by the 1770s it was being made in many parts of Japan. Tobe naturally adopted many of the Arita techniques.

Shards from the Kanbara and Kitakawage kilns reveal that the earliest porcelains here were plain white; later cobalt underglaze decorating techniques were transmitted from Nagayo and Hasami in Nagasaki Prefecture. Some beautiful cobalt-decorated pots exist with landscapes, bamboo grass, maple leaf, floral, and lattice motifs, and several excellent pieces from the earlier plain white porcelain period are extant. While earlier wares were hand-painted, in the late nineteenth century paper stencils had come into use, and these continued to be used after most potteries had adopted copperplate printing techniques with which to decorate their wares. Even after the end of the Pacific War, Tobe wares decorated with paper stencil motifs were made for export to countries in Southeast Asia. Cobalt-decorated tableware began to be mass produced; recently, however, plaster molds have been adopted in favor of wheel-thrown pottery. Today the Tobe potters are entering a new phase in which they work as artists, rather than craftsmen, and produce a new "folk" porcelain, mostly flower vases and tableware.

Tokushima Prefecture

Ōtani. Recent research has verified that the Ōtani kiln, situated to the north of Tokushima, was first built to fire porcelain in the 1770s. At present, it produces the biggest pots in western Japan, and the enormous garden bowls (*suirenbachi*), crocks, and persimmon jars standing in line in the sunny courtyard of this pottery is a thrilling sight. It takes two people to throw these big pots—one person lies on the ground turning the wheel with his feet, while the other forms the piece. First, the base of the pot is formed by coiling; then the walls are beaten with a paddle to thin them out and upwards. The last stage of forming consists of throwing the pot in the normal way.

The clay is fairly plastic, and pots are decorated in all sorts of different ways—from incising to applied and impressed designs—the latter used mainly on the rims of bowls and crocks to help compress the clay and prevent it from cracking during drying. Three patterns in particular are used—lightning (*raimon*), lotus, and chrysanthemum motifs. Potters make household altar candlestands, pouring bowls, chicken feed containers, lidded jars, wildflower vases, tea cups, and various other smaller wares, besides the huge pieces already mentioned. These are glazed entirely with strong iron glaze, chiefly a brown glaze made from a mixture of paddyfield clay and bamboo grass ash. Besides this, there is a black glaze that contains manganese, and occasionally unglazed pieces are fired. From the 1790s, potters started trailing saké bottles with household marks in white slip. They used to accept orders for large crocks from the Kansai area; until quite recently these were fired in large climbing kilns, which took five days and nights before the maturing temperature was reached.

Kōchi Prefecture

Nōsayama. On the banks of the river to the north of Kōchi Castle is a place called Ozu Odo. It was there that the local clan authorities established a kiln in the early 1650s. Much later, in the 1820s, the kiln was moved to Kamobe Nōsayama, where large deposits of clay had been discovered, and there porcelain wares, hardly distinguishable from those made at Tobe, were made. From the late nineteenth century, crocks, lidded jars, teapots, and kneading bowls, as well as grinding bowls, were fired. Nōsayama potters produced some particularly charming smaller wares, such as the green and brown glazed teapots and the white-slipped, round-bellied, large rice bowls known as *Gorōshichi*. The kiln site itself is located in a very pleasant part of the island.

Aki. The Aki kiln was located in Uchiharano, Aki city, in the eastern part of Kōchi Prefecture. It was set up in the 1820s by a potter who came from nearby Nōsayama and started firing all sorts of different pots, many of them being virtually indistinguishable from Nōsayama wares—wash basins, crocks, lidded storage jars, pouring bowls, *Gorōshichi* rice bowls, flat-based saké bottles, flower vases, green-glazed teapots, small teapots, saké warmers, saké bottles, grinding bowls, plates, casseroles, flowerpots, and so on. The most unusual of these is the round saké warmer known as *iraregan*.

SOME DECORATIVE TECHNIQUES

stamping

"feathering"

sprigging and glaze runs

slip inlay

straw whisk *hakeme*

stenciled decoration

"picture" (*e*) Karatsu

hakeme and finger wipes

1

2

3

4

5

OKINAWA PREFECTURE (1–9)

1. (*Preceding page*) Funerary urn. Tsuboya ware. Seventeenth century. 48.9 × 38.7 × 75.4 cm. Mashiko Reference Collection.

2. Tea jar, bull's-eye pattern. Tsuboya ware. Seventeenth century. H. 20.1 cm. Mashiko Reference Collection.

3. Votive flower vase, red clay and white slip. Chibana ware. Late sixteenth century. H. 18.8 cm. Japan Folkcraft Museum.

4. Hip flask, green and black trailed glazes. L. 20.1 cm. Tsuboya ware. Probably seventeenth century. Japan Folkcraft Museum.

5. Flower vase, incised decoration. Tsuboya ware. Seventeenth century. H. 11.1 cm. Mashiko Reference Collection.

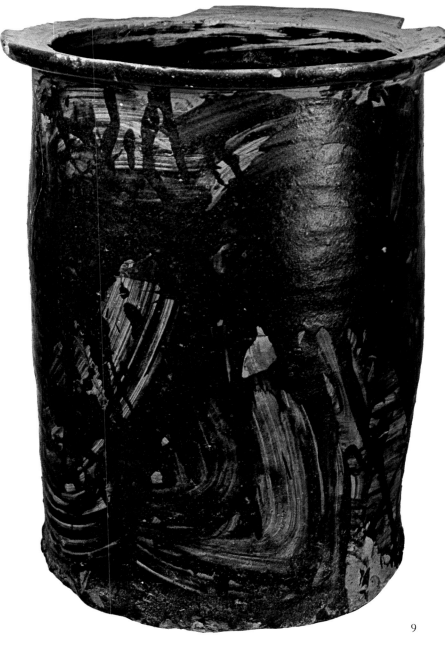

6. Dish, polychrome peony design. Tsuboya ware. Eighteenth century. D. 14.9 cm. Japan Folkcraft Museum.

7. Bowl, floral scroll design. Tsuboya ware. D. 24.6 cm. Japan Folkcraft Museum.

8. Foliate saké server. Tsuboya ware. Seventeenth century. D. 11.9 cm. Mashiko Reference Collection.

9. Urn, iron glaze. Kogachi ware. Middle sixteenth century. H. 44.8 cm. Mashiko Reference Collection.

KAGOSHIMA PREFECTURE (10–18)

10. Spouted saké bottle, celadon with trailed white glaze. Ryūmonji ware. Late nineteenth century(?). H. 15.3 cm. Kumamoto Folkcraft Museum.

11. "Sweet-saké" bottle, green and brown trailed glazes. Ryūmonji ware. Middle nineteenth century. H. 22.4 cm. Mashiko Reference Collection.

12. Household altar vase. Yokino ware. Eighteenth century. H. 30.8 cm. Kumamoto Folkcraft Museum.

13. "Sweet-saké" jar, modeled and applied plum blossom design. Naeshirogawa ware. Eighteenth century. H. 27.2 cm. Kumamoto Folkcraft Museum.

10

11

12

13

14

15

16

14. Buckwheat noodle bowl. Naeshirogawa ware. Modern. D. 14.7 cm. Japan Folkcraft Museum.

15. Bowl, chatter-mark decoration. Ryūmonji ware. Middle nineteenth century. D. 15.0 cm. Mashiko Reference Collection.

16. *Yamachoka* cooking pot. Naeshirogawa ware. Modern. H. 16.6 cm. Japan Folkcraft Museum.

17. "Sweet-saké" jar, incised decoration. Naeshirogawa ware. Seventeenth century. H. 30.4 cm. Kumamoto Folkcraft Museum.

18. Household altar vase, white slip decoration. Naeshirogawa ware. Eighteenth century. H. 26.3 cm. Kumamoto Folkcraft Museum.

17

18

21

KUMAMOTO PREFECTURE (19–22)

19. Square-shouldered saké bottle, running glaze. Shōdai ware. Middle nineteenth century. H. 21.8 cm. Kurashiki Folkcraft Museum.

20. Tea jar, slip inlay. Kōda ware. Eighteenth century. H. 42.1 cm. Kurashiki Folkcraft Museum.

19

20

21. "Boat" saké bottle, white trailed glaze. Shōdai ware. Middle nineteenth century. H. 20.4 cm. Kumamoto Folkcraft Museum.

22. Soy sauce crock, running glaze. Shōdai ware. Middle to late nineteenth century. H. 49.4 cm. Kumamoto Folkcraft Museum.

21

22

23

24

25

26

Imari Wares (23–45)

23. Saké bottle, cobalt underglaze, leaf design. Nae-shirogawa ware. Middle nineteenth century. H. 14.9 cm. Mashiko Reference Collection.

24. Saké bottle, brown glaze and incised decoration. Hirado ware. Middle nineteenth century. H. 26.5 cm. Kumamoto Folkcraft Museum.

25. Saké bottle. Hirasa ware. Middle nineteenth century. H. 21.3 cm. Kumamoto Folkcraft Museum.

26. Hexagonal saké server. Hirasa ware. H. 13.6 cm. Kumamoto Folkcraft Museum.

27. Small lidded box, polychrome overglaze enamels. Imari ware. Eighteenth century. 7.6 × 7.4 × 7.2 cm. Japan Folkcraft Museum.

28. Oil bottle, cobalt underglaze, peony design. Imari ware. Seventeenth century. H. 14.9 cm. Japan Folkcraft Museum.

28

27

29. Candlestick, cobalt underglaze. Imari ware. Middle nineteenth century. H. 14.6 cm. Japan Folkcraft Museum.

30. Square bottle, cobalt underglaze and overglaze enamels. Imari ware. Eighteenth century. H. 12.5 cm. Mashiko Reference Collection.

31. Hexagonal bottle, cobalt underglaze. Imari ware. Seventeenth century. H. 14.1 cm. Kurashiki Folkcraft Museum.

29

30

31

32. Cup, cobalt underglaze, bamboo grass pattern. Imari ware. H. 5.6 cm. Kumamoto Folkcraft Museum.

33. Tea cup, cobalt underglaze, wild chrysanthemum pattern. Imari ware. H. 5.2 cm. Japan Folkcraft Museum.

42

43

44

45

34. Cup, yellowish glaze stripes. Imari ware. H. 5.7 cm.

35. Household altar rice bowl, cobalt underglaze, lattice fence (*higaki*) pattern. Imari ware. H. 5.9 cm. Japan Folkcraft Museum.

36. Cup, cobalt underglaze, wave pattern. Imari ware. H. 5.5 cm.

37. Cup, cobalt underglaze, chrysanthemum pattern. Imari ware. H. 5.3 cm.

38. Cup, cobalt underglaze, iris design. Imari ware. H. 5.7 cm.

39. Cup, cobalt underglaze, impressed butterfly design. Imari ware. H. 5.7 cm.

40. Oil bottle, cobalt underglaze. Imari ware. Eighteenth century. H. 11.2 cm.

41. Plate, cobalt underglaze, cherry blossom pattern. Imari ware. Eighteenth century. D. 17.5 cm. Japan Folkcraft Museum.

42. Large dish, cobalt underglaze and overglaze enamels. Imari ware. Eighteenth century. D. 44.2 cm. Japan Folkcraft Museum.

43. Small cups, red overglaze enamel. Imari ware. Eighteenth century. Larger cup. H. 3.2 cm.

44. Bowl, iron underglaze, net pattern. Imari ware. Eighteenth century H. 5.2 cm.

45. Bowl, cobalt underglaze, impressed decoration. Imari ware. Eighteenth century. H. 5.6 cm.

46

47

49

48

Saga Prefecture (46–55, 74)

46. Bowl, white glaze splashes on black glaze. Karatsu ware. Seventeenth century. H. 8.7 cm. Mashiko Reference Collection.

47. Bowl, iron decoration. Karatsu ware. Seventeenth century. H. 9.8 cm. Mashiko Reference Collection.

48. Burial urn. Tatarō ware. Seventeenth century. H. 70.3 cm. Japan Folkcraft Museum.

49. Bowl, straw-whisk *hakeme* decoration. Utsutsugawa ware. Eighteenth century. H. 7.7 cm. Kumamoto Folkcraft Museum.

50. Saké bottle, finger-wiped slip decoration. Kuronda ware. Eighteenth century. H. 33.1 cm. Kurashiki Folkcraft Museum.

51. Saké bottle, brushed and patted slip decoration. Utsutsugawa ware. Middle nineteenth century. H. 29.8 cm. Kumamoto Folkcraft Museum.

52. Saké bottle, iron brushed decoration. Kuronda ware. Eighteenth century. H. 23.8 cm. Mashiko Reference Collection.

53. Saké bottle, brushed slip and chrysanthemum motif. Ōsotoyama ware. Eighteenth century. H. 28.8 cm. Japan Folkcraft Museum.

50

51

52

53

54

54. Kneading bowl, finger-wipe decoration and poured glazes. Ōsotoyama ware. Middle nineteenth century. D. 50.5 cm. Kumamoto Folkcraft Museum.

55. Large dish, millet motif. Ōsotoyama ware. D. 42.5 cm. Mashiko Reference Collection.

56

56. Lidded jar for pickled onions. Onta ware. Modern. H. 47.4 cm. Japan Folkcraft Museum.

57. Dish, brushed slip decoration. Onta ware. Modern. D. 16.2 cm. Japan Folkcraft Museum.

58. Large kneading bowl, poured glazes. Nishijin ware. Modern. D. 54.8 cm. Japan Folkcraft Museum.

59. Saké bottle, trailed wave design. Koishiwara ware. Middle nineteenth century. H. 23.3 cm. Mashiko Reference Collection.

57

58

59

60. Bowl, brown glaze and trailed decoration. Agano ware. Eighteenth century. H. 7.3 cm. Kumamoto Folkcraft Museum.

61. Large dish, poured glazes. Koishiwara ware. Modern. D. 59.0 cm. Japan Folkcraft Museum.

62. Saké bottle, trailed willow design. Agano ware. Middle nineteenth century. H. 26.7 cm. Kumamoto Folkcraft Museum.

63. Tea jar, poured glazes. Koishiwara ware. Middle nineteenth century. H. 43.5 cm. Kumamoto Folkcraft Museum.

64. Large altar vase, ash glazes. Nishijin ware. Middle to late nineteenth century. H. 22.1 cm. Kumamoto Folkcraft Museum.

61

62

63

64

65

66

69

67

68

70

SHIKOKU (65–73)

65. White chrysanthemum-shaped porcelain bowl. Tobe ware. Middle nineteenth century. D. 38.1 cm. Umeno Collection.

66. Herbal teapot, brown glaze. Nosayama ware. H. 9.7 cm. Japan Folkcraft Museum.

67. Rectangular household altar shrine, roof-tile clay. Modern. H. 23.7 cm. Kurashiki Folkcraft Museum.

68. Round household altar shrine, roof-tile clay. Modern. H. 23.8 cm. Kumamoto Folkcraft Museum.

69. Chopstick holder, incised decoration. Tobe ware. Middle nineteenth century. D. 10.5 cm. Umeno Collection.

71

72

70. Vase, incised decoration. Tobe ware. Middle nineteenth century. H. 20.5 cm. Umeno Collection.

71. Turnip-shaped saké bottle, slip-trailed calligraphy. Ōtani ware. Middle nineteenth century. H. 14.9 cm. Mori Collection.

72. Saké bottle. Ōtani ware. Middle nineteenth century. H. 36.5 cm. Mori Collection.

73. Large shallow dish, yellow *tenmoku* glaze. Ōtani ware. D. 68.4 cm. Mori Collection.

73

74

74. Large kneading bowl, mountain pine motif. Ōsotoyama ware. D. 51.1 cm. Japan Folkcraft
Museum.

Plate Notes

1. *Funerary urn. Tsuboya ware. Seventeenth century. 48.9 × 38.7 × 75.4 cm. Mashiko Reference Collection.*
Highly decorated pieces of this kind usually end up being rather detestable, and obviously some people might grow tired of looking at this sort of thing. Nevertheless, when Okinawans buried their dead, they felt that the least they could do was decorate the burial urn in which the ashes of the departed were put. It was not just sweat and hard work that went into this pot, but sympathy and respect. This work belongs to a world ruled by the spirits of the dead; it has taken over from that point where words can no longer express a man's feelings.

2. *Tea jar, bull's-eye pattern. Tsuboya ware. Seventeenth century. H. 20.1 cm. Mashiko Reference Collection.*
Hardly a rounder shape than this can be made with clay, and yet it has been given even further emphasis by the addition of a bull's-eye motif in white slip and iron oxide over another dipped glaze. One might well feel that this has made the pot almost too round. The form has been finished off with a small mouth, and the texture of the glaze is superb.

3. *Votive flower vase, red clay and white slip. Chibana ware. Late sixteenth century. H. 18.8 cm. Japan Folkcraft Museum.*
The iron-rich clay body of this vase has a beautifully calm sheen given it by the firing. The fact that it has a kind of skirtlike foot shows that the pot was made for religious purposes, as can be seen, too, in the lotus flower petal design on the belly. White slip has been faintly trailed from both lip and base of the bottle, giving its surface a hazy tone.

4. *Hip flask, green and black trailed glazes. L. 20.1 cm. Tsuboya ware. Probably seventeenth century. Japan Folkcraft Museum.*
This is a neat looking form, but it is typical of the Okinawan potter's character that its base should be made to look somewhat greasy. The lugs look a bit like old tree stumps, or dragon heads maybe, and certainly the fresh green glaze winding and wreathing across the surface of the flask resembles a dragon's body. This is a fine example of Tsuboya pottery, and is imbued with a dignity resulting from the tenseness of its form.

5. *Flower vase, incised decoration. Tsuboya ware. Seventeenth century. H. 11.1 cm. Mashiko Reference Collection.*
Small vases with broad stable bases like this one were probably placed in front of graves to hold flowers. The decoration is rather sweet and looks almost as if it were done by a child. A reduction firing has made the glaze slightly somber, but with superb tone. It was probably made at Tsuboya, although it is possible that it is Chibana ware.

6. *Dish, polychrome peony design. Tsuboya ware. Eighteenth century. D. 14.9 cm. Japan Folkcraft Museum.*
The bright but gentle peony design seems almost to be smiling out of the warm white-slipped background, giving the plate a sort of carefree tranquillity. According to written records, Okinawan polychrome glazing is Chinese in origin.

7. *Bowl, floral scroll design. Tsuboya ware. D. 24.6 cm. Japan Folkcraft Museum.*
Although present-day Tsuboya wares are said not to be as good as those made in the old days, if one looks really hard one can still find pieces like this. While this particular shape came into fashion from the late nineteenth century, potters at Tsuboya have been throwing pots for many hundreds of years. This is a really fine example of the "audacity" of Tsuboya wares.

8. *Foliate saké server. Tsuboya ware. Seventeenth century. D. 11.9 cm. Mashiko Reference Collection.*
This decorative form, with its incised, raylike decoration round the shoulder, has been dipped in a thick white opaque glaze, before having a bamboo grass motif trailed in manganese glaze. All this might have ended up making the jug look overdone, but the fact that the pot is imbued with great charm is typical of Tsuboya workmanship.

9. *Urn, iron glaze. Kogachi ware. Middle sixteenth century. H. 44.8 cm. Mashiko Reference Collection.*
The Kogachi kiln flourished during the late Muromachi period and was situated on the Motobu Peninsula. This urn is imbued with a feeling that can only be described as bold or audacious. Neither the shape nor the glazing of this pot would have been created in such marvelous fashion if the potter was meticulously concerned with the pot's function alone.

10. *Spouted saké bottle, celadon with trailed white glaze. Ryūmonji ware. Late nineteenth century(?). H. 15.3 cm. Kumamoto Folkcraft Museum.*
People living in Kagoshima, where Ryūmonji wares are made, are extremely fond of spirits, and this sort of bottle is a must for every household.

11. *"Sweet-saké" bottle, green and brown trailed glazes. Ryūmonji ware. Middle nineteenth century. H. 22.4 cm. Mashiko Reference Collection.*

The free-spirited manner in which glazes have been poured over the white-slipped and transparent-glazed pot makes this bottle look almost like a tree trunk entwined with creepers. This style of overglazing is known literally as "three-color" (*sansai*) glazing, but at times only two glazes are used. The tone of the slip here is superb.

12. *Household altar vase. Yokino ware. Eighteenth century. H. 30.8 cm. Kumamoto Folkcraft Museum.*

This vase has been given such a severe shape that it looks as if it has been made from steel rather than clay. The iron-rich clay body of the pot has been covered in a very thin rust glaze known as *shibukawa*. It is sufficiently thick enough for the vase to fulfill its function and gives it a certain carefree tone. Yokino wares come from the island of Tanegashima, between Kyushu and the Korean peninsula, and it was only after the Pacific War that it was discovered that pottery had ever been made there. A study of shards unearthed from around the old kiln sites on the island shows that all sorts of pots for everyday use were made there, some of them glazed, others not. Traces of shell are to be found in the shards.

13. *"Sweet-saké" jar, modeled and applied plum blossom design. Naeshirogawa ware. Eighteenth century. H. 27.2 cm. Kumamoto Folkcraft Museum.*

This large jar somehow reminds one of the burly torso of a country farmer. Its plum flowers blossom forth from the tips of slender shoots that have sprouted from a gnarled old branch. Heralds of the spring, they seem to be exuding a sweet fragrance from out of the dark depths of winter. The applied decoration may have been done especially to order, or perhaps on some whim on the potter's part—at any rate, there is hardly another design like it. This kind of crock is called a "sweet-saké jar," but it was probably put to a variety of uses and was not made to store saké alone.

14. *Buckwheat noodle bowl. Naeshirogawa ware. Modern. D. 14.7 cm. Japan Folkcraft Museum.*

This pot is slightly on the large size for a noodle bowl. It has been dipped in a thin glaze before having a thick brown glaze poured over it in various places, thus adding to the bowl's elegance.

15. *Bowl, chatter-mark decoration. Ryūmonji ware. Middle nineteenth century. D. 15.0 cm. Mashiko Reference Collection.*

Not many traditional old Ryūmonji pots survive today. Although this bowl looks at first glance to have been made in Onta, its light brown glaze is characteristic of Ryūmonji ware. The marvelous form of the bowl is beautifully set off by the rough chattering on its outside, while the strong wavy line of combed slip just under the inside rim gives the piece great charm. It is imbued with a freshness that can only come from having been used in people's everyday lives.

16. Yamachoka *cooking pot. Naeshirogawa ware. Modern. H. 16.6 cm. Japan Folkcraft Museum.*

This is a fairly small example of the *yamachoka* type of cooking pot. Its dark clay body has been glazed back, and a really solid looking spout and lug have been attached to it. It is said to have been used as a cooking utensil by people working in the fields, but what kind of food it contained is not known.

17. *"Sweet-saké" jar, incised decoration. Naeshirogawa ware. Seventeenth century. H. 30.4 cm. Kumamoto Folkcraft Museum.*

One's eye is arrested here by the way in which the body of the jar has been incised with a spray of iris leaves and one tiny budding flower. The fact that this single blossom looks so Korean in shape gives the pot a certain nostalgic melancholy, which the potters of Naeshirogawa must surely have felt—for they were Korean by birth, but were brought to live and work in Kagoshima at the very end of the sixteenth century. The incised decoration has a certain tenacity, which is not attained by present-day potters. Naeshirogawa black-glazed wares often tend to look dynamic and robust, but here both the glaze and the form of the pot are calm and peaceful.

18. *Household altar vase, white slip decoration. Naeshirogawa ware. Eighteenth century. H. 26.3 cm. Kumamoto Folkcraft Museum.*

Naeshirogawa wares were for the most part glazed black, but very occasionally, as here, white slip is used decoratively. The technique of applying the slip with the tip of one finger while turning the pot slowly on the wheelhead probably owes much to white Satsuma porcelain ware influence. At any rate, the pot has vitality, stature, and great composure.

19. *Square-shouldered saké bottle, running glaze. Shōdai ware. Middle nineteenth century. H. 21.8 cm. Kurashiki Folkcraft Museum.*

If it were not for the inwardly receding depth of this splendidly broad-shouldered bottle, it could easily be overlooked. The techniques used are simple enough, but they have been given a superb profundity in this lovely piece.

20. *Tea jar, slip inlay. Kōda ware. Eighteenth century. H. 42.1 cm. Kurashiki Folkcraft Museum.*

This tea jar has a form very reminiscent of Yi dynasty Korean porcelain wares—high neck and wide shoulders tapering down gently to the base. The technique of inlaying a clay body with slip is also Korean and was developed in that country in the Koryŏ dynasty (919–1392). It then came directly from Korea to the Kōda kiln and was assimilated into a Japanese style, which has here been perfected. To cover the whole surface of the tea jar in this manner required considerable skill.

21. *"Boat" saké bottle, white trailed glaze. Shōdai ware. Middle nineteenth century. H. 20.4 cm. Kumamoto Folkcraft Museum.*

This bottle has been given an exceptionally broad base so

that it remains stable if used aboard fishing vessels when they lift and plunge through the rough seas. It has been glazed in a sort of free-spirited manner. During the middle of the Edo period (eighteenth century), a number of Kyushu kilns developed the technique of pouring an ash glaze over the iron-bearing clay body and then trailing a second opaque glaze over this. The only kiln where this tradition has survived and is still practiced to this day is that producing Shōdai wares in Kumamoto Prefecture.

22. *Soy sauce crock, running glaze. Shōdai ware. Middle to late nineteenth century. H. 49.4 cm. Kumamoto Folkcraft Museum.*

Shōdai wares are thrown thick walled and tall then have an opaque glaze poured twice across their shoulders, giving them a robust nature. In the case of the crock illustrated here, there is not the slightest trace of that "ease" that this method of glazing can so easily convey, and one sees a really commanding piece of pottery.

23. *Saké bottle, cobalt underglaze, leaf design. Naeshirogawa ware. Middle nineteenth century. H. 14.9 cm. Mashiko Reference Collection.*

The leaf design in cobalt on the rounded body of this bottle has been rather roughly executed. This is a superlative and tasteful piece.

24. *Saké bottle, brown glaze and incised decoration. Hirado ware. Middle nineteenth century. H. 26.5 cm. Kumamoto Folkcraft Museum.*

This is one of a limited number of masterpieces from the relatively unknown Hirado kiln.

25. *Saké bottle. Hirasa ware. Middle nineteenth century. H. 21.3 cm. Kumamoto Folkcraft Museum.*

26. *Hexagonal saké server. Hirasa ware. H. 13.6 cm. Kumamoto Folkcraft Museum.*

Outstanding examples of plain porcelain are more frequently found among Hirasa, rather than Imari, wares. However, many of these are not at all widely known.

27. *Small lidded box, polychrome overglaze enamels. Imari ware. Eighteenth century. 7.6 × 7.4 × 7.2 cm. Japan Folkcraft Museum.*

This is a lovely little box that was fired in Kakiemon's kiln. The form and enameling are magnificent and made this box one of the late potter Kanjirō Kawai's favorite pieces.

28. *Oil bottle, cobalt underglaze, peony design. Imari ware. Seventeenth century. H. 14.9 cm. Japan Folkcraft Museum.*

The way in which this pot swells out full and round but yet remains light shows a healthy hand at work. The decoration has been done on a fairly large scale, and there is not the slightest trace of faltering in the brushwork.

29. *Candlestick, cobalt underglaze. Imari ware. Middle nineteenth century. H. 14.6 cm. Japan Folkcraft Museum.*

The thing that makes this piece so attractive is the fact that it is simple and was made to be used in people's everyday lives. The lines at the base of the candlestick are a bit uneven and casual.

30. *Square bottle, cobalt underglaze and overglaze enamels. Imari ware. Eighteenth century. H. 12.5 cm. Mashiko Reference Collection.*

The cloud forms borrowed from traditional Japanese painting at the top and bottom of the bottle have been adroitly combined with a single thick blossoming plum tree to form a splendid design.

31. *Hexagonal bottle, cobalt underglaze. Imari ware. Seventeenth century. H. 14.1 cm. Kurashiki Folkcraft Museum.*

This is an excellent piece whose form has been kept taut and decorated with an essentially Chinese pattern, digested and handled in a Japanese manner.

32. *Cup, cobalt underglaze, bamboo grass pattern. Imari ware. H. 5.6 cm. Kumamoto Folkcraft Museum.*

This selection of small pots (Plates 32–39) is typical of cobalt blue underglaze decorated porcelain (*sometsuke*) wares produced in Japan during the seventeenth and eighteenth centuries. *Sometsuke* was not, of course, the only type of decoration used, and one can find such other techniques as inlay, iron underglaze, and glaze pouring used on a wide variety of such forms. There was an almost infinite number of motifs used, and these exude a simplicity that makes it hard for one to put away a pot once one has started using it.

40. *Oil bottle, cobalt underglaze. Imari ware. Eighteenth century. H. 11.2 cm.*

It is not exactly clear what kind of leaves have been painted here as a decorative motif, but this mystery adds even further to the beauty of the pot.

41. *Plate, cobalt underglaze, cherry blossom pattern. Imari ware. Eighteenth century. D. 17.5 cm. Japan Folkcraft Museum.*

The brushwork on this plate is most inspiring, with a charmingly blurred effect in the cobalt lines and a ring of blue calculated to close off the whole pattern.

42. *Large dish, cobalt underglaze and overglaze enamels. Imari ware. Eighteenth century. D. 44.2 cm. Japan Folkcraft Museum.*

Imari ware became world famous because of its cobalt underglaze decorated (*sometsuke*) and overglaze enameled porcelain. This kind of decoration owes much to the *Yūzen* method of dyeing cloth and relies for its elegance on unbalanced patterns. The plate illustrated here is full of vitality and exudes a deep charm brought on by the combination of area, line, and color, the deep blue cobalt and white porcelain spaces. The four seasons are depicted. Pottery that combines the *sometsuke* cobalt blue and polychrome overglaze enamels is known in Japanese as *somenishiki*.

43. *Small cups, red overglaze enamel. Imari ware. Eighteenth century. Larger cup. H. 3.2 cm.*

These are simple and delightful pieces; the form is good and the enamel color comfortable to the eye.

44. *Bowl, iron underglaze, net pattern. Imari ware. Eighteenth century. H. 5.2 cm.*

This kind of net pattern is very common on Imari wares,

which are mostly painted in natural cobalt (*gosu*), but very occasionally, as here, in iron oxide pigment.

45. *Bowl, cobalt underglaze, impressed decoration. Imari ware. Eighteenth century. H. 5.6 cm.*
This sort of tastefully decorated impressed and cobalt-painted ware was made for everyday use by a number of kilns in Nagasaki Prefecture.

46. *Bowl, white glaze splashes on black glaze. Karatsu ware. Seventeenth century. H. 8.7 cm. Mashiko Reference Collection.*
This bowl is utterly subdued, incomparably tranquil.

47. *Bowl, iron decoration. Karatsu ware. Seventeenth century. H. 9.8 cm. Mashiko Reference Collection.*
The technique used here is known as "whale skin" (*kawakujira*) iron decoration, referring to the color contrast of a rim dipped in iron glaze. It is hard to find words to describe a marvelous piece like this.

48. *Burial urn. Tatarō ware. Seventeenth century. H. 70.3 cm. Japan Folkcraft Museum.*
The use of burial urns in Japan has great antiquity, and the urns naturally vary in design from one area of the country to another. The powerfully built form and the vigorous applied decoration bring to mind Jomon period (10,000–300 B.C.) pottery. The way that the urn has been thinly glazed makes the piece seem to wail like a ghost in the wind.

49. *Bowl, straw-whisk* hakeme *decoration. Utsutsugawa ware. Eighteenth century. H. 7.7 cm. Kumamoto Folkcraft Museum.*
Although this bowl is commonly identified as Utsutsugawa ware, it in fact may well have been fired at Mikawachi. The fanning waves of the slip decoration applied with a straw whisk are carefree and give the pot great beauty.

50. *Saké bottle, finger-wiped slip decoration. Kuronda ware. Eighteenth century. H. 33.1 cm. Kurashiki Folkcraft Museum.*
This magnificent piece has been given an almost overwhelmingly dynamic movement by the slip decoration, which itself contrasts beautifully with the full but subdued form of the bottle.

51. *Saké bottle, brushed and patted slip decoration. Utsutsugawa ware. Middle nineteenth century. H. 29.8 cm. Kumamoto Folkcraft Museum.*
The quiet yet wild effect of this special slip decoration technique is very appealing.

52. *Saké bottle, iron brushed decoration. Kuronda ware. Eighteenth century. H. 23.8 cm. Mashiko Reference Collection.*
This bottle could hardly have a more classically correct form or simpler design with which to decorate that form.

53. *Saké bottle, brushed slip and chrysanthemum motif. Ōsotoyama ware. Eighteenth century. H. 28.8 cm. Japan Folkcraft Museum.*
This is a famous piece, unparalleled for its calm dignity.

54. *Kneading bowl, finger-wipe decoration and poured glazes. Ōsotoyama ware. Middle nineteenth century. D. 50.5 cm. Kumamoto Folkcraft Museum.*
One of the attractions of the Ōsotoyama kilns is the size of the wares made there. There is an enormous quantity of bowl and crock shards to be found around the old kiln sites, and over half of these have finger-wipe decorations and green and brown overglazing. This makes it virtually impossible to estimate how many thousand pots like the one illustrated here were fired during the kiln's three centuries of active production.

More than fifty kilns all told seem to have fired this particular type of kneading bowl. All sorts of finger-wipe decorations were tried, before potters fixed on this particular one with its radiating lines near the rim of the pot and multiple rings at its center. Since almost all bowls were shipped to their ultimate destinations, they had to be made almost paper thin. This may not seem demanding, but in fact it requires consummate skill on the part of the potter. As with the following illustration, the exact origin of this bowl is unclear because of the large number of kilns active in Ōsotoyama.

55. *Large dish, millet motif. Ōsotoyama ware. D. 42.5 cm. Mashiko Reference Collection.*
This, like the dish illustrated in Plate 74, is a famous example of Ōsotoyama ware. The edge of the dish has been combed to produce a wavelike effect, and the rock and millet stalks have also been combed while the white brushed-on slip was still wet. Millet stalks are also brush painted with iron oxide and green glaze. Despite the variety of techniques used here, one does not feel that the potter has tried to be too impressive. The dish has a certain calm power, without being overwhelming, and is expansive in a serene way. It is difficult to judge from which of the kilns this particular piece came. One guess is that—together with the dish illustrated in Plate 74—it was produced before the pictorial designs of the Yumino kiln became stereotyped, which would date it probably before the Genroku period (1688–1704).

56. *Lidded jar for pickled onions. Onta ware. Modern. H. 47.4 cm. Japan Folkcraft Museum.*
There are few few pots indeed that can rival the neatness with which this jar has been first slipped, then decorated with chatter-marking (*tobiganna*), before having large controlled splashes of green and brown glaze poured over its shoulders. The way in which the main body of the jar swells out from the base in a curve that is echoed by the roundness of the lid is quite beyond verbal description; this piece evokes the very heart of Japanese folkcraft.

57. *Dish, brushed slip decoration. Onta ware. Modern. D. 16.2 cm. Japan Folkcraft Museum.*
This brush (*hake*) decoration is characteristic of Onta wares. Pieces are brushed all over with thick slip immediately after being thrown on the wheel. The potter then slowly turns the wheel by hand and pats his broad *hake* brush onto the surface of the pot, so that an umbrella-riblike pattern

emerges. The warm streak of brown overglaze poured over the transparent glaze gives the plate even greater charm.

58. *Large kneading bowl, poured glazes. Nishijin ware. Modern. D. 54.8 cm. Japan Folkcraft Museum.*
The rim of this bowl has been given great vigor by the thickly poured black, brown, and white overglazes. The form of the pot is majestic and has been given warmth by the ash glaze. This is a superb example of the special style of Nishijin ware.

59. *Saké bottle, trailed wave design. Koishiwara ware. Middle nineteenth century. H. 23.3 cm. Mashiko Reference Collection.*
In contrast with the pot shown in Plate 62, this bottle has been heavily reduced during firing, so that the glaze is mottled. Although Koishiwara is located far inland, the wave decoration has been applied with considerable skill. It is almost impossible to find saké bottles of such superb quality being made today.

60. *Bowl, brown glaze and trailed decoration. Agano ware. Eighteenth century. H. 7.3 cm. Kumamoto Folkcraft Museum.*
The form of this bowl suggests that it was probably used for drinking something hot, like soup. The trailed decoration is made from powdered stone, not slip.

61. *Large dish, poured glazes. Koishiwara ware. Modern. D. 59.0 cm. Japan Folkcraft Museum.*
The poured glazes give this dish remarkable power. This technique would appear to have been used at Koishiwara for more than two hundred years, for shards unearthed at old kiln sites there show that bowls and plates fired long ago were glazed in precisely the same way.

62. *Saké bottle, trailed willow design. Agano ware. Middle nineteenth century. H. 26.7 cm. Kumamoto Folkcraft Museum.*
This superb piece came out of an extremely oxidized firing. Its lustrous brown glaze has a design superbly trailed in slip of two willow branches.

63. *Tea jar, poured glazes. Koishiwara ware. Middle nineteenth century. H. 43.5 cm. Kumamoto Folkcraft Museum.*
The beauty of this piece derives from the vigor of the swelling body of the jar, from the thick lugs, and from the splendid glaze, which has blistered during firing.

64. *Large altar vase, ash glazes. Nishijin ware. Middle to late nineteenth century. H. 22.1 cm. Kumamoto Folkcraft Museum.*
This piece has a classic, if somewhat heavy looking, shape, whose ears jut out with great firmness. The form tends to be somewhat cold, but it is mellowed by the warmth of the glazes.

65. *White chrysanthemum-shaped porcelain bowl. Tobe ware. Middle nineteenth century. D. 38.1 cm. Umeno Collection.*
It is often thought that the Japanese do not really appreciate white porcelain for its color, but prefer to emphasize different forms to the detriment of design. This is a magnificent work whose generous, rippling body is given a tautness by the chrysanthemum shape of its rim.

66. *Herbal teapot, brown glaze. Nōsayama ware. H. 9.7 cm. Japan Folkcraft Museum.*
Such pots are made of refractory clay that will not break over a naked flame and were used to brew herbal infusions and as kettles for hot water. The lightness with which this pot has been made shows the skill with which a trained potter can throw any number of pieces exactly alike. It also reveals, along with the thinly poured glaze, that this piece was made to be sold cheaply. It was just an ordinary teapot sold at a general store in Kōchi during the early Shōwa period (mid-1920s to 1930s), which anybody could buy for a few pennies.

67. *Rectangular household altar shrine, roof-tile clay. Modern. H. 23.7 cm. Kurashiki Folkcraft Museum.*
This small shrine would look very much at home under a wayside tree. The cedar smoked surface of the piece has begun to peel away, giving it a slightly golden sheen, and the roughly hand-formed square shape makes the shrine look somewhat portly, but greatly composed.

68. *Round household altar shrine, roof-tile clay. Modern. H. 23.8 cm. Kumamoto Folkcraft Museum.*
Hardly a simpler form than that of a flat top, cylindrical body, and rectangular base exists, and it is certainly one at which one never grows tired of looking. The surface of this pot is almost as black as lacquer and exudes a certain peaceful strength. While such roof-tile ware was almost certainly made somewhere along the coast of the Seto Inland Sea, the exact origin of this piece remains unclear.

69. *Chopstick holder, incised decoration. Tobe ware. Middle nineteenth century. D. 10.5 cm. Umeno Collection.*

70. *Vase, incised decoration. Tobe ware. Middle nineteenth century. H. 20.5 cm. Umeno Collection.*
The incised decoration on this vase may have been added to give a feeling of tautness to the area where the foot rim meets the belly of the pot. The decoration in Plate 69 is of fresh grass leaves, and that in Plate 70 of Japanese bush clover; both decorations have great charm.

71. *Turnip-shaped saké bottle, slip-trailed calligraphy. Ōtani ware. Middle nineteenth century. H. 14.9 cm. Mori Collection.*
This is a marvelous shape known as *kabura* ("turnip"). The way in which the pot ascends into great swelling shoulders fully reflects the hard work that went into it. The character for *saké* has been freely trailed with a bamboo slip trailer over the thick reddish brown glaze.

72. *Saké bottle. Ōtani ware. Middle nineteenth century. H. 36.5 cm. Mori Collection.*
This bottle has been given magnificent firmness by the way in which its lower part tapers. During firing, the fine-grained surface of the clay became pitted in several places, and this gives the effect of a cluster of fireflies gleaming out of the overall somber dark brown glaze.

73. *Large shallow dish, yellow* tenmoku *glaze. Ōtani ware.*
    D. 68.4 cm. Mori Collection.

This dish has been given a wonderfully relaxing effect by the way in which a glaze made from paddyfield clay and bamboo grass (*sasa*) ash was applied overall and then the same glaze trailed once more before firing. Although it is frequently asserted that modern potters cannot produce such powerful works as this, it is fair to say that in fact they still do so in places like Ōtani.

74. *Large kneading bowl, mountain pine motif. Ōsotoyama*
    ware. D. 51.1 cm. Japan Folkcraft Museum.

The gnarled pine tree enclosed by the circumference of the large wheel-thrown pot is truly striking. The brushstrokes outlining the budding freshness of the green branches and radiating out from the pinecones are a red brown. Forming a background to this most basic of color contrasts is a thick white slip, which over the years has mellowed in color and infuses the bowl with a hazy tranquillity. Such epithets as "majestic" or "dignified," so frequently used to describe other works of art, fade into nothing when applied to a work of this stature. One could almost say that here lies revealed the very spirit of the pine tree, pulsating with vigor and life.

Folk Kilns of Kyushu

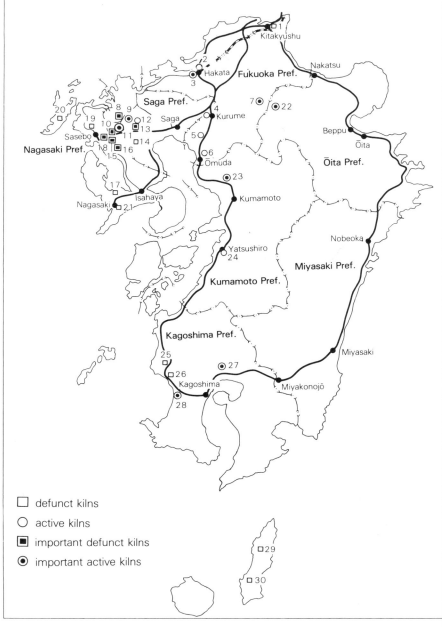

1. Agano
2. Noma
3. Nishijin
4. Shiraishi
5. Akasaka
6. Futagawa
7. Koishibara
8. Shii-no-mine
9. Tatara
10. Harayake
11. Arita
12. Kuronda
13. Ōsotoyama
14. Kamino
15. Kiharayama
16. Hasami
17. Nagayo
18. Mikawachi
19. Sasa
20. Nakano (Hirado)
21. Utsutsugawa
22. Onta
23. Shōdai
24. Kōda
25. Hirasa
26. Kushikino
27. Ryūmonji
28. Naeshirogawa
29. Yokino
30. Noma

□ defunct kilns
○ active kilns
▣ important defunct kilns
◉ important active kilns

Folk Kilns of the Arita Area

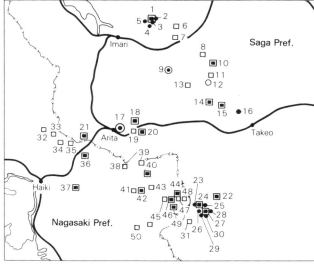

1. Shii-no-mine	18. Yamabeda	35. Jizōdaira
2. Kami-tatara (Upper Tatara)	19. Mukurodani	36. Enaga
3. Naka-tatara (Middle Tatara)	20. Hyakkengama	37. Mikawachi
4. Shimo-tatara (Lower Tatara)	21. Harayake	38. Furusarayashiki
5. Shingama	22. Yumino	39. Hatanohara
6. Fujingawachi	23. Teikihara	40. Muragi
7. Kanaishibaru	24. Niwagi	41. Sarayama
8. Yakiyama	25. Umenokihara	42. Hie
9. Tatarō	26. Yazaa Valley	43. Uchinomi
10. Kawago	27. Kodaji	44. Nagao
11. Sabi Valley	28. Kashinokiyama	45. Seiji
12. Kuronda	29. Shimomatsu Valley	46. Nakao
13. Mukaiya	30. Shirakibara	47. Kōrai
14. Taitani	31. Uchinoyama	48. Kibayama
15. Kotōge	32. Yanaginomoto	49. Sannomata
16. Sakurantōge	33. Yoshinomoto	50. Atemuki
17. Arita	34. Annomae	

Folk Kilns of Okinawa

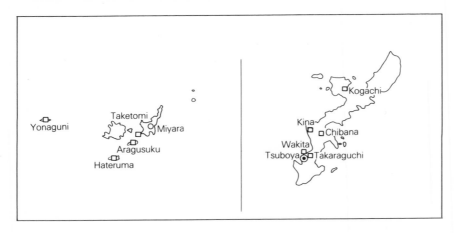

Folk Kilns of Shikoku

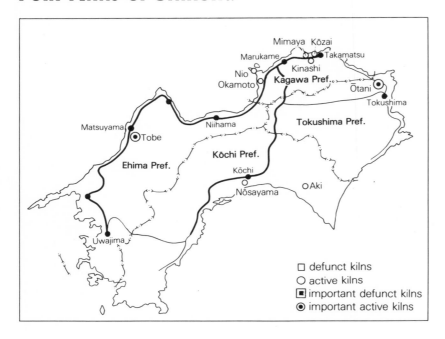

定価2,900円

in Japan

DATE DUE

RESERVE

DEMCO 38-297